# THE SECRET OF ACADEMIC PROGRESS AND SUCCESS

## Education that is Christian

# AUDU SUYUM

Revival Waves of Glory Books & Publishing
PO Box 596
Litchfield, IL 62056
https://www.revivalwavesofgloryministries.com/

Published in the United States of America

Paperback: 9781980575658

# TABLE OF CONTENT

# INTRODUCTION

We all cherish great men and women from every field and profession in life. When we read or hear about successful personalities from any profession, we thrill at them, celebrate them and we even can tabulate their stories and sincerely wish ourselves were those people. Unfortunately, we often seem less concern about the secret of their success. We just do not care to know their secret than we busy "worship" and wishing to be like them.

What is the secret of academic progress? Or is it a gift given to some few individuals? Can celibacy, marriage, family and environment affect academic progress? Well, I believe the libertarians, economists and the motivational speakers of our day who strongly believe in the uniqueness and capability of man will never allow us draw to an end that academic progress is a gift to some few. Man, what he needs is strategic plan. Progress and success are not much about ability for man already is able but careful planning. Men who fail in life are those who, perhaps could not planned well!

Success is a matter of methodology and strategy. This is clear justified in the many "how –to" books maintaining and discussing ten, fifteen, twenty keys of ..., ten principles or laws of ..." such is the postmodern theory of progress and success.

But is this true? Is success just a matter of careful planning? Is academic stand-still lack of planning – planning of the time table, for example? It is not in the scope of this booklet to debate all the questions, however, I must acknowledge that planning certainly has its place in progress and success of any kind but it can never be central factor. It is always a secondary matter.

The secret of progress and success, let me quickly put it in a passing respect, is determination. Determination is the inertia energy or impetus that sets every genuine, every ordinary being on motion and journey to success. Men of determination can always and almost keep advancing and attend success without much planning as such. When men are determined for something, it cannot be an exaggeration to say that nothing in heaven or on earth could be a barrier. No, not even God! when David was determined to delight in and meditate on God's law, rejection, mockery, trouble and distress could not stop him (Psalm 119:13a, 141, 143); when Joshua was determined to walk with God, the majority could not convinced him (Josh. 24:15), when Daniel and friends were determined not to worship idol, the fiery finance and the lion den could not appall them (Daniel 3:16-18, 6:10); when Nehemiah was determined for the rebuilding of the temple and the broken wall of Jerusalem, Tobiah and Samballat could hardly stop them; when Ezra was *determined* for Studying, keeping and teaching God's Law, family affairs and the situation of time could not stop him (Ezra 7:10); when the primal people were *determined* for a democratic government and city of Tower, only God could stop them. All these men may not have had expertise knowledge on strategic planning, yet they succeeded. The secret of their success is determination. If we are determined like them, school fees are hardly an issue.

You may ask: What then is determination? Fine! Determination in a general sense is a conviction of certainty on something that calls for complete attention, time and resources gladly expend on without regret and complain but rather count it all joy, privilege, and an investment. To put it differently perhaps more explicitly, what you are determined for gives you joy and satisfaction and so you joyously dedicate your life for it to an extend it becomes your God or god!

How can one be determined? One will be determined if he/she lives to discover the ultimate goal of his existence and the particular gift and calling he has, and decided not to envy others but become himself and best in his/her little world of service. Thus in this way he/she affects the whole world. This is because concentration is power – the energy you need to progress and succeed.

# **PREFACE**

The reason for and purpose of this booklet is to seriously warn against what I called "Certificate Knowledge", explain true learning and to address some academic challenges most students seem to face in their academic pursue regarding how to balance spirituality and academics and how to be diligent in studies. This I do, not as an expert but as a student who feels and concerns for others and wishes to do the best he could to help his fellow students understand and solve their problems as well as escaping the danger I have seen ahead. The problems of academics are too much problems to be life for the experts alone! As much as one understands and can help his other fellow in his trouble one is encouraged to help. After all, speaking like a Christian, the Bible says we should carry the burdens of one another (Gal.). Certainly, I consider it a burden to help to have taken this risky decision to write on this subject.

For this reason therefore, I acknowledge every mistake – grammatical or otherwise as my own and sincerely apologize for whatever offence that might have caused you. After all, perfection is a process. It comes gradually through lot of mistakes, anyway.

Actually, as you may have noticed from the "two chapters" of this booklet are independently different from each. I have decided to put them as chapters under the general heading *the secret of academic progress* because they are independently too little a work to be published on their own. However, taking them together provide an insight to the overall title of the booklet. I regret that I am unable to write a kind of "how-to" a book on the subject as many of you might have expected, and I am afraid if there is something like that. So if you are coming with such an intention, you may possibly be disappointed.

This booklet is written therefore primarily for my fellow students on campus who as mentioned earlier are concerned with their spirituality and academics but do not know how to maintain both without doing harm to the other and those who are perhaps possessed with the academic disease (virus) - "the GPA mentality". This does not mean that other persons cannot benefit from it if the wish to read.

# CHAPTER ONE

# THE STUDENT AND ACADEMIC VIRUS: GPA MENTALITY

Sound health, strength and vitality are necessary for academic progress and success. No student can hope to succeed without health. It is necessary and therefore important. It is a priority.

Regretfully enough, virus, a tiny infectious pathogen is almost all over the world affecting all forms of life – yes, even academic life! As it is no surprise to think of computer virus, so also academic virus that I called "The GPA Mentality". It is such a fatal disease that whoever wants to succeed in life and academics must learn to take preventive measures against it.

## WHAT IS GPA MENTALITY?

The GPA mentality, like love, is hard to define in a word or sentence other than to describe and or explain. Nevertheless, the GPA mentality, to put it simply, refers to a state and time when the thinking faculty of students and lecturers is predominated with desire and anxiety for GPA in so much that their lives and lifestyles become characterized by the thought (the GPA thought) where until is not seen as "good" but absolutely necessary for academic success and success in general at which point it becomes a value system of life. It is a state when students are no longer interested in learning to transform themselves but to show; it is a state when learning becomes a mere tradition and a lane or alley to obtaining certificate; it is a state and time when people study not to learn but secure certificate reading first class. The fact that most students could go no further than class lectures and read no wider than lectures' Hand-Books is clear proof and symptom of the heinous disease.

Students spend time drifting around talking and boasting or regretting of their GPA scores and nothing else – something they could scarcely prove it in their lives and speeches. It is not found in their hearts but on their heads only but for a few moment because it (the knowledge) was forced to be only during the so-called period of examination as they put no effort to learn thereafter and even when they manage to read, the read only the AC (Area of concentration)! What a mess! When learning is no more but to pass examinations and to obtain certificate? Is not this (the GPA mentality)? Indeed, an academic virus reducing and restricting learning to class setting thereby relaying only on lectures' Hand-Books and when by any chance, he goes to the library is to solve assignments, and again reducing the goal of education to certificate. Is the goal of education certificate? How have we fallen victims of this virus, the GPA mentality? That then is the disease. What is the cause?

## THE HARMFUL EFFECT OF THE VIRUS

### 1. The Stress Factor and moral evil

Given a conducive environment, every virus is capable of replicating itself until it dominates the host and destroy it. It is sad to hear and see that the GPA mentally has brought about academic competition which also in return has led to stress and emotional breakdown of many students, heart-attack, ulcer, blood pressure (BP) and many other related diseases. Certainly, hard work and "overworking" in calm spirit do not break down a person than envy, competition and anxiety do. Surely they are dangerous healthy lifestyle. People should learn simplicity.

Consistent desire for high GPA score has let many students to steal in exams, practice sharming or collect power from devil just to know everything, bribe lectures to be favored and earn more marks, hate themselves as the other person is making better than the other. Yes, they may even kill! What a mess!

### 2. Mechanical Student

Perhaps the most pernicious effect of the GPA mentality is that it leads to being mechanical, never original never yourself. Students are always restricted to thinking their own way, speaking and writing their own way, speaking and writing their own ideas but in some old traditional outdated stuff passing on from one generation to the other, and also restricted to the ideas, method and wish of their lectures, and they remain loyal to this just because they want to make high GPA score.

The result? They become mechanical – always repeating what other have said and done for long – never having ideas their own. Oh what a ridiculous practice! Whatever is done by force cannot give good result. Man is not a robot but a free being. Godly freedom is what defines and sets man different from other creatures. No true learning without freedom – freedom to think, to speak and to write your way. Learning is not a dictatorship but a guide – guide to straight thinking, guide to sound judgment, guide to moral living guide to putting one's best. That is learning. That is education.

### 3. Ineffectiveness

No man should hope to be productive who is not himself. It is no surprise that we have countless number of "learned" persons in this generation than ever before but there is no tangible change and transformation in our lives, moral values and society. Most are just mechanical people repeating abstract ideas and ideologies that are irrelevant to us. All they could show and boast of is their certificate, the real knowledge and ability to impact life is absent. Are not these the miserable and most detestable people of the society who worship "Belly God?" unfortunately, our society wants such people – people with certificate without knowledge to give them joy, to give them support but rejecting and forgetting the true ones.

Such is the trouble of our society. But woe unto them that call good evil and evil good (Isa. 5:20).

## CAUSES OF THE VIRUS: THE GPA MENTALITY

Every learned and faithful doctor knows that proper treatment of any complication requires a carefully trace of the parthenogenesis of the disease. In the same way, in order to offer reliable answers and suggestions as solutions to this problem, we must know first its causes.

What are the causes of the GPA mentality? One could see and list many causes, however, I have three things/factors of which I believe to be the basic cause of the virus and these are:

### 1. The Society

Perhaps Dr. Jiddu Krishnamurti is right to observe that men have created a society that we in turn have become its slaves. (Krishamurte 1-29). We seem to be imprisoned and controlled by our culture than we order our culture ourselves.

Our moral codes and value systems are determined or justified by majority or the world-view of a given society. Certainly, the social anthropologists would see nothing wrong in this as they insist that man cannot be human being outside his culture. This is true at least, in a sense. But when a man is enslaved by his culture rather than the opposite, then we are no more human beings other than robots. That is the problem.

We live in a society that certificate reading high GPA score is become the secret of progress and success – academic success, economic success, political success, marital success. One cannot proceed to BA without secondary school certificate nor one can proceed to MA or PhD without strong GPA. Again, one cannot secure good job or aspire for any leadership position without it nor find a beautiful wife without certificate! If you also want promotion in your work-place, just enroll for another degree to obtain another certificate! Men and women are defined and measured by educational certificates. What we were and what we are and what we shall be is already recorded on the certificate. We are our certificates! The ability and dignity of human beings are measured and written on a paper certificate.

The implications of this view and practice of education or learning process cannot be mentioned especially on those who have no access to education. Depression, frustration, hopelessness, emotional break-down suicide, wrong choice, rebellion and terrorism are all likely to be the defining features of the lives of these categories of persons. For they are not only regarded as third-class citizens by the certificate holders but also as the most useless, miserable, unwanted beings and detestable sinners.

Consequently and of course, unfortunately, education becomes a competition not in a sense that people want to learn but just to obtain certificate and become recognized and popular in society. We are all liable to this tendency and the worse is that we have easily succumbed to it. Most students are therefore controlled by these world standards of competitive life pride and arrogance in their view and approach to education. And since learning is not their ultimate concern but certificate, they become keys in their studies putting no effort to reading wide. This is how our society has affected our education and our dignity.

## 2. Academic Lecturers

Lecturers too greatly contribute to the cause of the disease as they keep frightening students with their exam questions. Their lectures are exam oriented in so much that they could not emphasis a point but for exam purpose and encourage no students to study but for assignment and examination. In fact I am sometimes very much offended to hear lecturer going to the extreme of shamelessly telling his/her students that their future is in his/her hands. What he means is that he can decide to pass or fail the student, and if he passes him, the student has future but if not, doom and hopelessness. Such claim is not only academically dangerous but morally and psychologically destructive.

Lecturers usually fall into this error for lack of competency in the knowledge of their subjects or lack of leadership ability to lead or a way of retaliating students for offence they might cause him. I must humbly confess that I already read a lecturer off the time he is emphasizing a point for the sake of exam.

Students get scared and have to restrict themselves to "him". This is pitiful indeed, that lecturers themselves are missing the point. But every serious student must learn to "fight" this issue.

### 3. **Psychology**

There is such a subject the experts called educational psychology that concerns with the scientific study of the learning process thinking to approach learning in an objective manner and putting all on scale for experimentation. The result is the intelligent quotient (IQ). Human intelligence is measured on paper by asking some abstract questions that are already hinted to students either in form of lecture or AC! The memorized and crammed disconnected ideas a now recorded as students' intelligence and sadly enough, the students are complacent with this assuming they know something and that is true intelligence. In doing this, the educators assume, in some concept to test the students true intelligence as he (the lecturer) grades him (the student) pass – a proof to the lecturer that the student understands him and his lectures in the class whereby at a point lecturers and educators consider it a motivation too for the student to put his best. But this is not true as the whole practice becomes nothing but a barrier to education, relationship as it produces envy, competition and pride in the student's life.

If I must be frank, I must confess that there is nothing I consider devilish than this useless and so-called practice of measuring intelligence. Can intelligence be measured? Is text or examination a true text of intelligence? Is the person's morality taken to consideration? Is the person's skill considered? Are the factors surrounding him at the time of examination regarded? What is intelligence but the whole of man? Can you truly measure man's intelligence as you neglect other values of the person? Is man a cramming being? Can there be true knowledge without character? Is not that a theory, an abstract idea without true bearing and impact on one's life? There will be no academic progress and success whatsoever as long as we keep holding and incarcerating ourselves in this devilish ideology.

I completely consent with Daniel R. Marsh when he writes:

> Education should make us live life with Zest, with gusto, with exuberance. But so much that passes for education takes away the wonder of life, and puts us in deadly peril of things named and classified. So much that passes for education is only the smoke of futile fire that has done nothing but consume life. The reason is because so much that passes for education lacks the most important element (Rebar 19)

> That is the point all, what is supposed to build and equip us for a higher purpose and function, we have turned it a fire to consume and destroy us. Shame!

# CHAPTER TWO
# TREATING THE VIRUS

Having seen the disease, its scandals and its causes, we turn now to considering solutions to the challenge without which the aim of this chapter is actually defeated. For there is no point spending time to describing a problem without attempting to solve.

To overcome this problem, let me kindly assert that it is absolutely necessary we redefine and reinterpret the meaning, nature and goal of education but we may need to write a complete book on this alone if we have to do so.

In a passing respect, education is a learning process whether formally or informally, independently or dependently. It starts from birth to death. Its nature is such that is flexible. Its ultimate goal is to first develop the learner, a person as he works to develop others in return – not to provide him certificate! If education, in our definition is good, then it must first build goodness in the learner first, for I agree with krishnamurti that we are the world. What that means is that our cultures and value systems are nothing but exact reflection of who we are. If we inculcate good in people, the result of their actions will definitely be good, at least. But as long as we motivate and stir people to learn just to obtain certificate that will provide them good name and popularity, we are bound to fail. We must campaign against all the complex educational systems and policies of our time if we want progress. People who truly know what education is must agree with Paul Bergevin when he writes:

> The sooner we can adjust our system of education to people instead of trying to adjust people to our education system; the sooner will strike a blow advancing the civilization process.

> Life is more than a frenzied scramble to earn money, to possess more, bigger and better things (Bergevin 97-99)

We must emphasis this fact because the ultimate goal of education is to provide freedom – godly freedom, to make someone creative, responsible, productive and maturing beings on earth. It is to help a person, the learner discovers himself – his talents, strength, weakness and ways to overcome them and his relationship with others. It is to guide the learner attends a certain degree of happiness and satisfaction in life. To summarize in the words of Michael R. Peterson, "It is to provide the mind with life and shape the whole person" (Peterson 13).

But alas, how we have succeeded turn it into a lethal weapon! When we talk of education is power and light, we have in mind certificate with which we will secure jobs and positions. People without the certificate are the unlearned. But we have forgotten that education is a process of learning achieved either formally or informally. If this is true, why do we always regard the certificate holders as more important than those without? Does it necessarily mean that one is a learned simply because he attended some so-called organized structure, kept in a class, restricted to some incompetent lecturers may be, for some few years? What about the rest of the time? Is not learning for life-time? Do we mean that the things the person is learning outside the class and so-called gorgeous building are no learning? Why then do we always think of the certificate holder and the learner at home as if their difference(s) is both in kind and degree? Is not this a mistake? Surely William Boyd got it right:

> The instrumentality, controls, or richly documented insights and predictions of highly professional users of education as we already know them were out of the ken of even the most visionary of past educational. So the growth of public educational institutions and policy make the past's gentle oasis of pedagogical theory a mirage. At least, it is so

describable in so far as it has failed to heed the harsh needs of the present, the imminent perils of the future, and the immense distance to be covered by realistic practice.

Besides, social science shows that even the learning theory and select in processes of the early and twentieth centuries were just as caught up in the social assumption of their time as Plato's prescription in fourth century B.C- misjudging what was observed, ignoring such now obvious factors as the social engagement of intelligence or maturation or indeed of the whole personality, and overlooking the need for constant evocation of everyone throughout life on a multiplicity of points. It was perilous to ignorance matrices of education even if society had been relatively static, but the prospect of automation, successive occupational retraining, and lifelong readjustment in a society of universal urban expectation all make the speculation and proto-technology of early twentieth centuries educators as logically outmoded as house maids and copy- clerks. They exist, but they are largely an anachronism and mainly because of technological and social change (Boyd vi-vii).

After all, Alfred North Whitehead writes, "A merely well informed man is the most useless bore on God's earth" (Whitehead 1)

## Discipleship: True Learning: The Greeks and the Past Education

Whether we like it or not, know it or not, modern and postmodern men owe great thanks to the Greeks. We can never talk about the western education that we are so much proud of without tracing its origin to the Greeks. It is no exaggeration that William Boyd writes:

> The proper starting point for a study of educational beginnings which aim at an understanding of our own times is in Greece, the motherland of our civilization. At the name of Greece, as Hegel said, the modern cultured man feels at home. His religion, that which is transcendent and distant, has come to him from the east, and especially from Syria, and there is always something strangeness about. On the other hand, what is present, science and arts, all that makes life satisfying, elevates and adorns, it is derived directly or indirectly, from Greece. The dept. with regard to education is only part of large dept., and it is not the least (Boyd 2)

It is obvious from the history of their education that they never schooled to earn certificate but to be equipped and make a difference and positive change in life. The ultimate goal of their education was to be a man of word (speech) and action (virtuous conduct). To achieve this, they looked after soundness and competent tutors who can train a disciple like himself and of course, more than himself! This they did because they understood the secret and the fact that the level at which a student could go and perform depends largely on who his tutor is. All the great philosophers we celebrate today were at a time greatly influenced by another influential philosopher either in person or through the philosopher's writings. They accepted the person's teachings and happily lived his life. This is true education – discipleship.

When Plato listened to Socrates, he became his disciple; when Aristotle listened to Plato, he also became his disciple; When Phillip listened to Aristotle, he ordered him to be a tutor to his son, Alexander the great; when Zeno read of Xenophon's memorabilia of Socrates, he asked of a man like him that he may become his disciple and was directed to Crates the cynics (Ferguson 354). This has been the practice until the end of nineteen century. All these men looked up to their disciples because they had something to offer them and their disciples rejoiced in that their disciples kept their names, beliefs, ideas, works, and contributions in memory for generation everlasting.

The truth is, there shall never be a successful student with tremendous impact without true disciple. Unfortunately, scholarship education is lost in the scientific approach to education that is purely objective in both content and context thinking to avoid being responsible for its teaching. Teachers only pass on ideas and facts that are there never making claim of one as his own.

This is utter foolishness!

Every true teacher that teaches must teach something that is his own, that himself cherishes and will encourage others to do the same. If we see education as discipleship, then every disciple must have something wonderful he wants others to know it to live it and die it. The concern here is not that you have got a message, an idea – a transforming idea to pass a cross. You want your disciple to believe and practice your beliefs and practices; you want him to be like you in every aspect – in life, action, profession. The Greeks did not mind certificate reading some useless mathematical figures that is called GPA. And as they were not affected by this virus, they put their best and leaved a memorial mark on the history of mankind. Knowing the value of education, they turned it to a public matter.

Unless we learn to see education this way, we will never make any tangible and lasting impact in life but to continue exploiting ourselves and our world.

## In a world coming of age

In a world coming of age, we will sooner or later no longer need the useless, empty and perishable papers called certificates. For then we might have all got certificate(s) with the rate of competition in education today. If this happens what else have we got to show and brag about? Early before now, a primary and secondary school graduate were considered the most learned and respectable person in the community. But when people began to obtain diploma, degree and masters' certificate, no body regards the secondary graduate again. Today if you have first degree (BA) it is as if you never gone to school yet considering the number of academic graduates. And the master and PhD will soon be a common thing. Then I shall see with what we shall use to employ people, to make name, to dub people to power and to deceive others.

In this era of globalization, what we need is a living and working certificate that is a person instead of a paper. Certificate, in my view, should record the time, duration of and place where somebody has schooled.

We should mature enough to put off childish things (Phil. 3:4b-14).

**Baptism in the Library**

**Academics & Spirituality**

The purpose of this chapter is to answer the question on the relationship between academics and spirituality and the implications (the question) it has on students especially in a college where rigorous and vigorous studies is encouraged

**The Question**

Students, especially Christian students who have been faithful, committed and devoted in their Christian lives when they enter college and are bogged down with academic exercises, they soon become confused and keep asking: **How Can I Adjust to Keep Balance Between my Academic and Spirituality?** This experience is usually astonishing and really intensifying to them who usually assume that Christian and Bible colleges, Seminaries and Universities are meant to study Bible and the Bible alone. Either way, and for whatever reason, people who are sincere with their spiritual lives and always with to be in tune with God have seldom escape the question of keeping balance between academics and spirituality.

**Adding on to the Problem: The Error of Dualism**

Not only students, lecturers, too expressed concern for the right balance between academics and spirituality. I have lived to hear lecturers addressing Christian students who have just come in for studies, that Colleges are academic grounds, and if one is not already grounded in faith and be careful, he/she will lose the faith. Therefore, students should be careful with the kind of lectures they receive, the books they read in and from the library. They must ensure they keep their academics and spirituality at the same rate or else the aim of their coming here is defeated.

Certainly that is a good fatherly and pastoral council and I know for certain that the lecturers are being honest in doing so but whether consciously or unconsciously, they already given a view and impression that academics and spirituality are two independently different practices. Students who hold to this view live in constant inner crisis – the crisis of concern to reconciling academics and spirituality. Such is the danger of dualism

What is the way out? Well, that is what we will now turn to look at. However, I must confess the difficulty of this problem and its controversial nature and therefore beg to say I have no adequate answer as one may think. What shall follow as an answer to this is nothing more than an attempt from my understanding and personal experience or testimony in a sentence or so.

## Answering the Questions: Considering the Meaning of Academics and Spirituality

Why have we come to a state of looking at academics and spirituality as enemies constantly waging war against each other and who need some judge to reconcile them? The simple reason is our understanding of the meaning of the two, I believe. What are academics, and what is spirituality?

Academics, as generally assumed, is an abstract game of ideas and words in the air without any practical relevant on people. It is just a task of building and developing theories.

But before I proceed on, permit me ask but a question. If this is our view of academics – nothing more than theories, why then have we ventured to take the risk of coming only to play the same game of ideas and words up there in the air knowing we want to effect practical change and transformation in the lives of people? Can abstract ideas help achieve your goals? Why not go elsewhere that practical matters are taught? Why college – a ground of academics? If academics has nothing to add up on our spirituality and living, then we certainly have deceived and cheated ourselves to have spent our money and time in a college where academics is its focus.

Spirituality, on the other hand, is seen as some cultic exercise that requires some sacred environment where one will spend some minutes, hours or days reading the Bible and praying and or active participation in church activities such as Bible study, fasting, Youth Fellowship, New Life For All, Youth Band, Women Fellowship etc. One who spends time in the library and scarcely participates in those things is regarded as the ungodly. According to this view, spirituality means escape from reason and reality (separation and isolation) but engaging in asceticism and activism

But one cannot take long to condemn this view and practice of spirituality as utter nonsense and preposterous. From just a cursory reading of psalms 1.3. True spirituality is meditated. That does not sound like activism and asceticism in the first place. It concern first with the exercise of the mind – thinking, pondering, considering and inquiring net, in the words of krishnamarti, by "withdrawal into a monastery, or into a room, sitting quietly for ten minutes or an hour, trying to concentrate, to learn to meditate, and yet for the rest being a hideous, ugly human being" (Krishuamerti 19).

Spirituality is not ignorance

The reason why we feel empty and blame that at academics is because we have false view and practice of spirituality as referring to spending sometimes alone or with others in a seclusion reading and praying the Bible. That is all. But spirituality is not ignorance. In fact true spirituality is true and correct  understanding – understanding of God and plans for man and his environment and issues without this knowledge, people always perish throughout the bible, God keeps emphasizing on being and understanding before doing (Hosea 4:6, Mt. 7:24). Hearing, listening (understanding) first before doing when we turn this topsy-turvy, the result is always a crisis and contradiction.

Academics are an inquiring into deeper and higher knowledge and understanding that will transform and conform lives. It is never meant to destroy spirituality but to build it. For it **is absolutely impossible to be spiritual without understanding** and academics are the effort put to seeking the understanding. For what is spirituality without sanctification? And will there be sanctification without understanding? SURELY NOT! The theology of sanctification is the true understanding given by the Holy Spirit whereby it transforms our lives by the renewing of our minds. Roms.12-1:2, Phil. 3:10, john 17:3.

Let the world proves me wrong I will humbly and gladly apologize and change my position. The truth is one and worth saying. There is no true spirituality whatsoever but in and through academics, inquiry into knowledge and understanding. Christians must stop holding to some empty and endless religious traditions that add no value to our being and development but concern only with mystic experience without knowledge (John 4:20). For what is spending minutes, hours, days, weeks, months and years reading the Bible, praying and fasting and doing all the activities – all out of religious respectability – to do to me without understanding? Are not all but mere and empty religiosity? Unless we learn to extirpate religious respectability, we will keep living a fragmentary and scattered life without meaning and taste.

As for me, the library is the "pillar and ground" of baptism, sanctification and true spirituality. For one cannot be spiritual without knowing what is going on neither can one be a human being without being criticized and or confirmed. History has five lessons to teach – to correct, criticize, warn, confirm and humble as it reminds you that others have gone ahead of you and your ideas in life and said and done what you want to and about doing. There is nothing new on earth, indeed.

As I read others, I learn new things, I have my ideas checkmate, my perception of things (including God and men) and issues criticized and have to think again, my aspiration and deeds confirmed and I rejoice and finally, I'm warned of repeating the same mistake others have done and as a result, I become adjust and matured in thoughts, judgment (reason), speech, relationship and actions. I'm shaped and become better person. Things I used to hold to and practice, I volitionally let go without using force on me. I become responsible in my life and dealings with God and fellow human beings. This is true spirituality, true academics.

As a matter of fact, I have never prayed as I ought to until I'm making studies. It is hereupon that I may sometimes be convinced of my errors and cannot proceed on until I confess before God; it is hereupon that I receive confirmation and rejoice in my heart, making melody as I praise God; it is hereupon I will see the need for others and pray to God to act; it is hereupon I'm warned of mistakes and encouraged to live a better life before God and men. After all, it is in the library I got baptized!

While I cannot overemphasize this fact, it is important to say that I'm not here totally condemning solitary studies, prayers and some church activities but simply saying that there is no difference between academics and spirituality in the true meaning of the two, and an even if we think there is (or which there is not), academics (understanding) must come first before activities. Activity never builds and transforms a life than it wastes it.

If we still cannot accept this, then there is no meaning whatsoever to leaving your beautiful and secured house, your great family and relations to going into a college sleeping on a tiny bed, sharing rooms without privacy and paying huge amount of money into the college account only for the college to destroy your spirituality with some mighty force of abstract ideas without practical bearings? What for? Is not that a waste and a big lost? Or have we come into college just to receive certificate? Then, that is the worse.

We should learn to value learning for its eternal importance to and for human development at every level and aspect of life NOT for any reason other than this. No, not even the certificate you will receive at the end. For lack of knowledge (ignorance in general) of any kind is extremely destructive.

The danger is not a right balanced between academics and spirituality as we think. The problem is the temptation of going to the extreme.

**The need and necessity for diligent studies: facing the challenges of the time**

Every old and new born of the twenty first century knows well that the time of waiting on the Holy Spirit without personal preparation has passed even as that was practiced in ignorance. Inadequate knowledge of the Bible and issues an around us have always led to shame and disrespect of the preacher as he remains a boredom to the congregation. There is no doubt that pastor turning to some psychological gimmicks in worship is nothing but sheer sign of inadequate knowledge. No learned preacher could do such things. Good communication skill is different from psychological gimmicks.

According to Paul in 2 Tim 2:15, correct interpretation of scripture requires proper understanding that comes from diligent studies or else we keep doing injustice to the text, deceiving and causing harm on people and shame to ourselves and the name of God. One cannot expect to be faithful to Bible interpretation without putting to diligence in studies. And we should know, it is to our own judgment to be unfaithful in the interpretation of the Bible and handling of God's people (Jer. 23:25-32). Certainly, to be lazy in studies as a minister of God is already a sign of unfaithfulness. God and I can forgive at least, the aged but not youths who are still strong but like drifting about doing nothing – yet claiming the call of God to serve! That is a pity.

Beside this fact that we need diligent studies for correct interpretation of the Bible, it is also true that we are living in an age of rational skepticism, scientism and madness, and these groups doubt the claims and practices of religion especially the Christian religion, and these are the same persons you are called to pastor – they are before you in the congregation. How do you help address them and their problems to affirm their faith in God when you do not know what they know and are talking about? Or do you mean to condemn them and their ideas as evil just because the Bible says ……….. ? That is force and wrong use of authority, then.

If the gospel means anything to us, and as faithful custodians of the gospel, will have to defend the gospel as we answer anyone who asks us the reason of our hope (1 pet. 3:15-16). We cannot but take the risk to know what the people know and the perspective from which they are coming from, until this is done, we will lose them to hell forever. Whoever considers their lives important must work hard to knowing and doing something on their situation. We must come to a point of confessing that religion and science, faith and reason are no enemies but faithful partner helping each other to victory as one cannot do without the other.

Moreover, science and technology have invented things that have turned to destroy our dignity and value systems. How can we as faithful ministers of God address these issues without understand precisely what the issues are all about? And how can we understand them without putting to diligence?

The truth is that if we want to be faithful in our interpretation, if we want to build and benefit the faith of our members, if we want to answer them asking us skeptical questions in and about our faith, if we want to address and solve the problems of our time, if we want to be respected as ministers, if we want to honor God, if we want to bless the world, we just have no option, no choice but to bend to studies, to learn to be disciplined and be diligent in our studies. Diligence is the way to go, the only means to be productive in life and ministry. It is in thin way and in this way alone God is glorified, men are saved, souls are edified and the world is blessed. Yes, even the next generation. There is no option; there is no alternative but one – diligence – diligence in studies.

We must put our best to do our best and transform the world for best and better. For this is the only opportunity and time we have in this life and again the only reason and purpose of existence and survival on earth till date – to impact lives, change the world for better. This is God's glory and honor, and our blessings. (Eccls. 9:10, 12:1-13).

Put your best! Put your best!! Put your best!!! And that is your success!

# NOTES

Boyd, William and Edmund J. King. *The History of Western Education.* London: Adam and Charles Black, 1975.

Ferguson, Everrete. *Backgrounds of Early Christianity.* Grand Rapids, Michigan: WB Eerdmans Publishing Company, 1987.

Krishnamurti, Jiddu. *You are the World.* New York: Harper and Row Publishers, 1972.

Lebar, E. Lois. *Education that is Christian.* England: Victor Books, 1989.

Peterson, L. Michael. *Philosophy of Education.* Leicester, England: Inter-varsity Press, 1986.

Whitehead, North Alfred. *The Aims of Education.* New York: The Free Press, 1929.

# OTHER BOOKS BY AUDU, SUYUM

SPIRITUAL DEPRESSION

UNDERSTANDING CREATION

WISDOM FOR LIVING